BOLD KIDS

Ancient Rome

ANCIENT HISTORY BOOK FACTS AND PICTURES FOR CHILDREN

If you want to teach your kids about the history of Rome, then you can read these Facts about Ancient Italy for kids. The first capitol in the city was located on the Capitoline Hill, which was home to the emperor's palace and the gods' temple.

Many words from Ancient Greek and Latin have been adapted into modern English, such as the months of the year and the word for sofa. Children can learn about the different food habits of the Romans, as well as the strange habits of their rulers. In the first century, they used to eat flamingo, and they ate dinner sitting down on couches.

The Romans were amazing architects and engineers. They built walls and roads, and they also learned art and business. They even built aqueducts to carry water to public baths and toilets.

They also worshipped many different gods, including Saturn, Zeus, and Jupiter. In addition, they ate by using their hands, and rarely used knives. They tended to eat exotic foods, and the rich were known to sacrifice animals to worship their gods.

PIVS·IX·PONT·MAX

In addition to being amazing architects and engineers, the Romans were also extremely innovative. Their cities were constructed entirely of stone, and they were inhabited by multiple families and relatives.

Aediles were responsible for collecting taxes and maintaining public buildings and festivals. These individuals had to be aediles in order to be consul, and they could even throw people out of the household. In addition to building structures, they also held massive festivals to make themselves popular.

The ancient civilization of Rome was home to many wonders. The city was built by two brothers who were nursed by a she-wolf. They later became the capital of the Roman Empire. During this time, there were no middle classes.

The ruler of the city was the father. The father owned everything in the house, including the children. Women had a limited amount of freedom, though they could work outside the home.

The first film in history was made by Trajan's column. This ancient structure was covered with statues, and the Senate appointed them to rule each city. It was an important part of the Roman empire.

Its rulers were responsible for collecting taxes, building public buildings and festivals, and keeping records of the citizens. In addition to this, the ancient Romans had many different gods. One of the most famous is the goddess Venus.

In the second century, Rome became a thriving city. The Forum was the center of the city, and the people sang carmen to celebrate each occasion. In the arena, the senators ruled the city.

They had many public baths, and the Tiber river was the source of all their water. The Romans were influenced by the Greeks and influenced their music, and the Romans also listened to the natural melodic sounds of songs.

Romans worshiped many different Gods. They had a variety of religions. They were the first civilizations to use writing to express their beliefs. The Romans also had many great soldiers, and the world was at their feet.

They were very intelligent and had a vast understanding of the ancient world. These were the first people to build a city that would last for hundreds of years. But the people of Rome were different from the Greeks.

Romans were amazing architects and engineers. They built roads, walls, and aqueducts. They even had the ability to speak Greek and Latin, and they were among the first to use written communication.

Their food was very diverse and often was eaten with their hands, so they did not need to use knives or forks. However, Romans were some of the most skilled fighters in the world. These facts about Ancient Rome for kids should be studied in high school.

The Romans were incredibly clever. They developed roads, walled towns, and more. Their cities had the first cinema in history. They were famous for their public baths.

They had a postal service. They also had streets and a lot of statues. They had a street cleaner and a fireman, and they had a postal service. Ultimately, they were the greatest architects and engineers of all time.

CPSIA information can be obtained
at www.ICGtesting.com
Printed in the USA
LVHW070529041022
729903LV00008B/93

9 781071 708736